Inside or Outside

Where's Eddie?

Daniel Nunn

Illustrations by Steve Walker

Raintree

Chicago, Illinois

Hide and Seek

www.capstonepub.com
Visit our website to find out more information about Heinemann-Raintree books.

To order:
☎ Phone 800-747-4992
💻 Visit www.capstonepub.com to browse our catalog and order online.

Edited by Dan Nunn, Rebecca Rissman, and Sian Smith
Designed by Joanna Hinton-Malivoire
Picture research by Mica Brancic
Originated by Capstone Global Library, Ltd.
Production by Victoria Fitzgerald

Library of Congress Cataloging-in-Publication Data
Nunn, Daniel.
Inside or outside : where's Eddie? / Daniel Nunn.
p. cm.—(Hide and seek)
Includes bibliographical references and index. ISBN 978-1-4109-4713-0 (hbk.)
ISBN 978-1-4109-4719-2 (pbk.)
1. Vocabulary—Juvenile literature. I. Title.
 PE1449.N775 2012
 428.1—dc23   2012000356

Acknowledgments
We would like to thank the following for permission to reproduce photographs: Shutterstock pp.5 (© loriklaszlo), 6 (© Thanida), 7 (© Elnur), 8 (© Kletr), 9 (© Adam Fraise), 10 (© Ihnatovich Maryia), 11, 12 (© tkemot), 13, 14 (© Marteric), 15, 16 (© ansem), 17, 18 (© Ivonne Wierink), 19, 20 (© Patricia Hofmeester), 21 (© jocic), 22 (© WebStudio24h), 23 (© Lois M. Kosch).

Front cover photograph of a tent reproduced with permission of Shutterstock (© vichie81).

Every effort has been made to contact copyright holders of any material reproduced in this book. Any omissions will be rectified in subsequent printings if notice is given to the publisher.

2

Contents

Be careful when you hide!
Eddie can hide in places where people can't. Hiding inside things can be very dangerous. Always ask an adult if it is safe first.

3

Meet Eddie the Elephant

This is Eddie the Elephant.

Eddie loves to play hide and seek!

Inside

Sometimes Eddie hides **inside** things.

When you are **inside** something, you are in it.

Outside

Sometimes Eddie hides **outside** things.

Outside is the opposite of **inside**. When you are **outside** something, you are not in it.

Find Eddie!

Can you find Eddie?
Count to 10, then off you go!

10

Where is Eddie? Is he **inside** the tent or **outside** the tent?

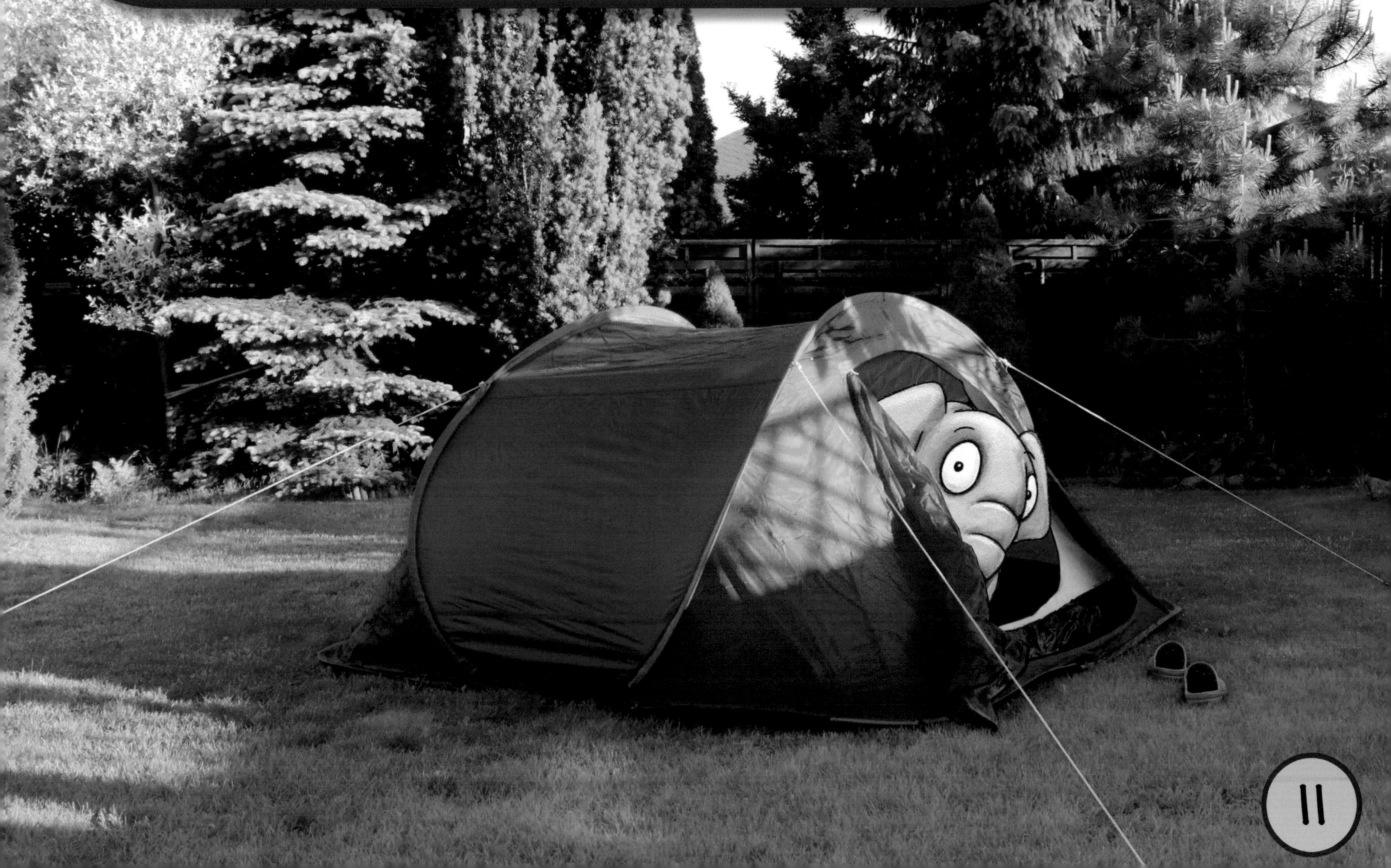

Eddie is **inside** the tent.

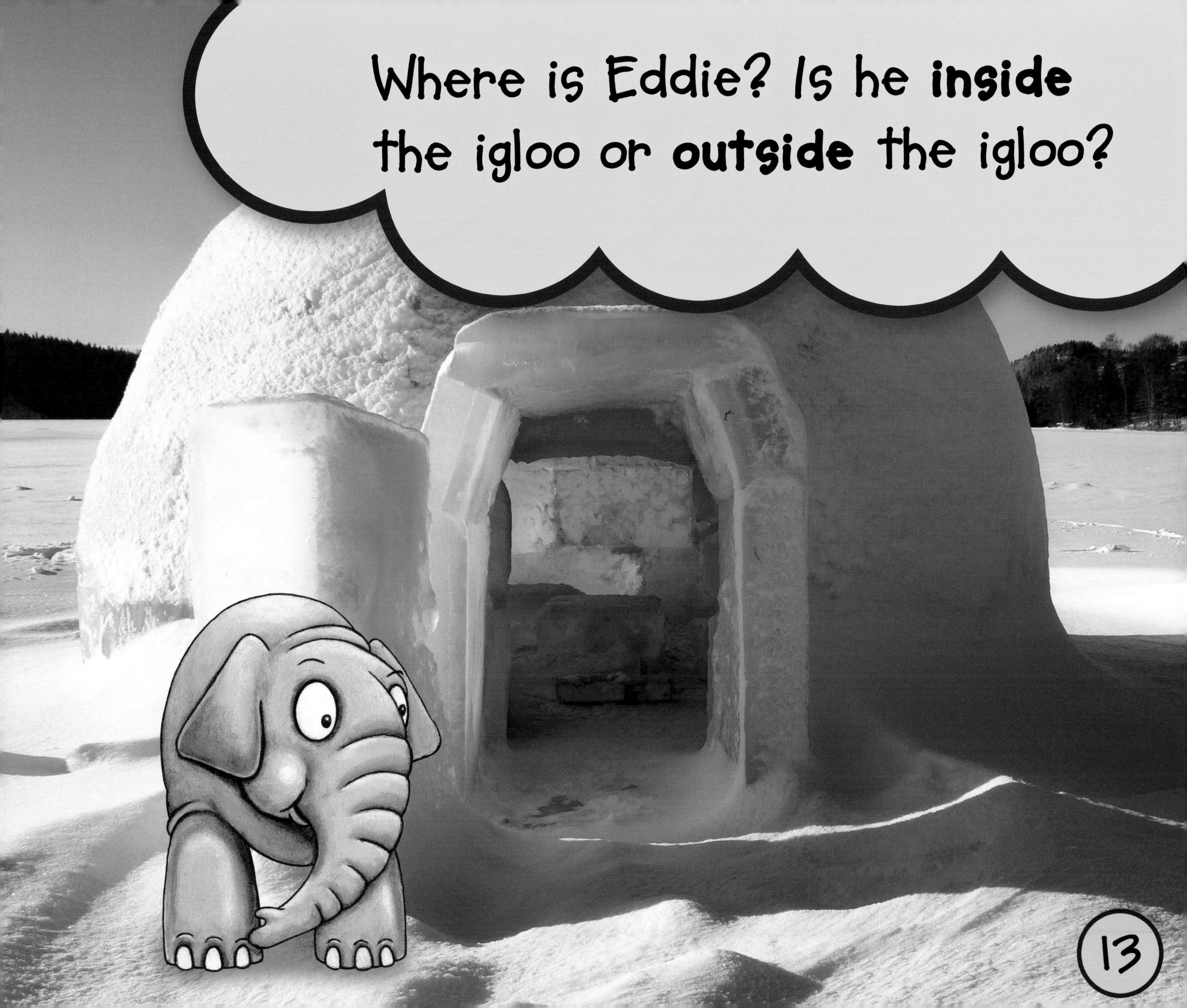
Where is Eddie? Is he **inside** the igloo or **outside** the igloo?

Eddie is **outside** the igloo.

14

Where is Eddie? Is he **inside** the helicopter or **outside** the helicopter?

Eddie is **inside** the helicopter.

Where is Eddie? Is he **inside** the cupboard or **outside** the cupboard?

Where is Eddie? Is he **inside** the suitcase or **outside** the suitcase?

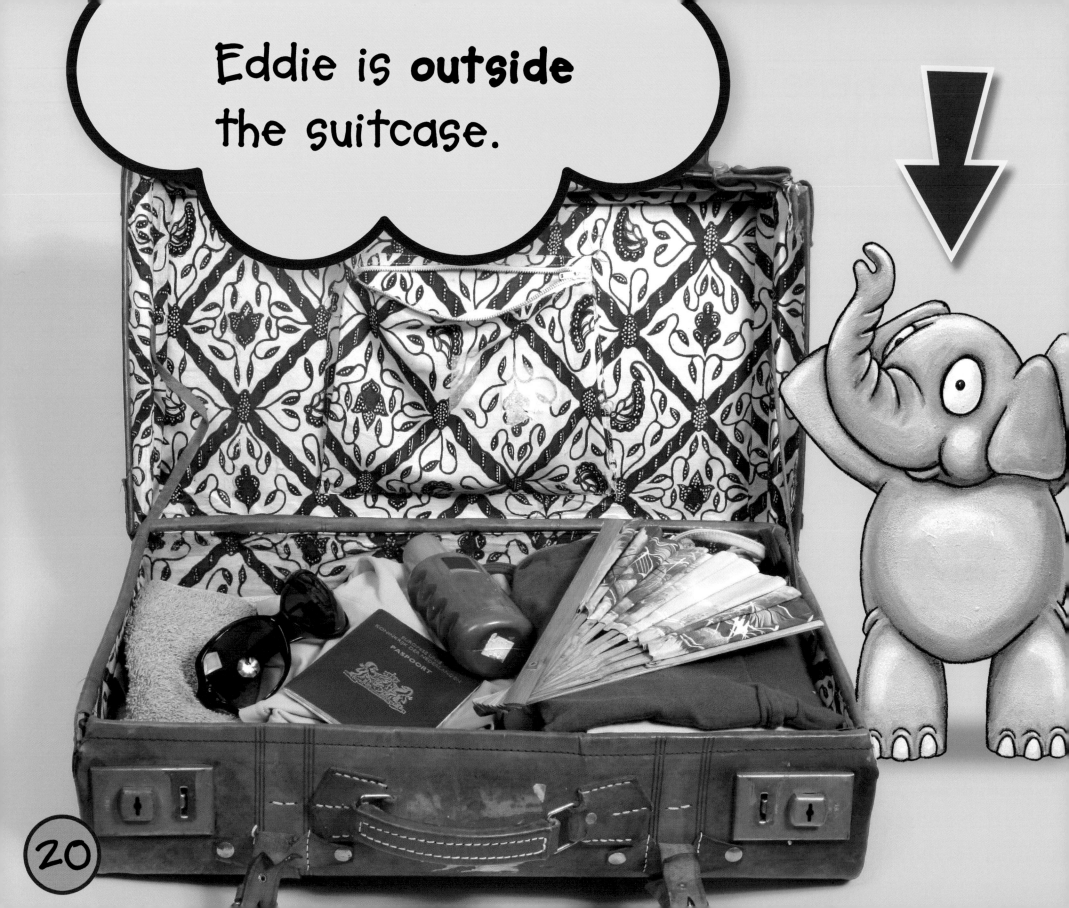

True or False?

1. Eddie is **outside** the shoe.
   True or false?

You can find the answers on page 24.

2. Eddie is **inside** the playhouse. True or false?

22

3. Eddie is **inside** the rocket.
True or false?

Answers and More!

True or false?

1. False! Eddie is **inside** the shoe.
2. True! Eddie is **inside** the playhouse.
3. False! Eddie is **outside** the rocket.

Where can Eddie hide next?

Look around the room you are in.

What could Eddie hide **inside** of?

What could Eddie hide **outside** of?

Hide and Seek

Inside or Outside

Where's Eddie?

Can you find Eddie the Elephant?
Is he inside or outside the house?

About the author:
Daniel Nunn has worked as an author and editor of children's books for many years. He enjoys playing hide and seek with his two young children, but he is not as good at hiding as Eddie the Elephant and they always find him.

Books in the **Hide and Seek** series provide an entertaining introduction to words that tell us where things are. This book looks at "inside" and "outside." The fun, cartoon-like design combined with the interactive "hide-and-seek" approach makes these books visually appealing for young readers and great to read aloud together.

Titles in the **Hide and Seek** series:
In Front Of or Behind: Where's Eddie?
Inside or Outside: Where's Eddie?
Left or Right: Where's Eddie?
Near or Far: Where's Eddie?
On or Under: Where's Eddie?

About the illustrator:
Steve Walker has been drawing creatures of all shapes and sizes ever since he could pick up a pencil. He lives near Oxford with his wife, daughter, and two goldfish. When he's not drawing he enjoys cooking and going to the movies.

Language Arts

Heinemann Raintree

a capstone imprint   www.capstonepub.com

ISBN 978-1-4109-4719-2